Original title:
Thistles and Theories

Copyright © 2025 Creative Arts Management OÜ
All rights reserved.

Author: Hugo Fitzgerald
ISBN HARDBACK: 978-1-80566-657-8
ISBN PAPERBACK: 978-1-80566-942-5

Seeds of Doubt

In the garden of questions, we sow,
With every tiny seed, a new doubt will grow.
Who knew sunshine could tickle the mind?
And weeds of confusion are all you can find?

Roots of uncertainty dance in our heads,
While pondering flavors of blue raspberry spreads.
A flower named 'Maybe' tugs at my sleeve,
While logic grins slyly, 'You'll never believe!'

Entangled Ideals

Two lofty ideals met under a tree,
Swapping tall tales of what's 'supposed to be.'
One sprouted giggles and silly old dreams,
While the other shot out plans with wild schemes.

They tangled their branches in whimsical ways,
Bouncing off thoughts like they're part of a play.
"Should we plant roses or simply just jest?"
"We'll flip a coin, but what if it's dressed?"

Chasing Shadows

With giggles and glee, we follow a shade,
Where sunlight goes dancing, just look at it flayed!
One shadow declared it was genius, of course,
The rest of us chuckled and followed the horse.

A hill gave a hiccup, a cloud played peek-a-boo,
As laughter erupted like popcorn anew.
And who would've guessed that shadows could lead,
To adventures of nonsense, just follow your creed?

Unyielding Posies

In a patch of posies, the bravest will shout,
Their petals are fearless, no room for a doubt.
They wear crowns of sunshine and giggle in rows,
Debating the weather as each flower grows.

"Let's dance in the rain, or wave at the sky!"
They twirled with a wink, as the bees buzzed close by.
And though storms may come, they refuse to be downed,
These merry posies will always rebound!

Labyrinth of Leaves

In the park, I took a stroll,
Got lost again, it's my main goal.
My map, a salad, tossed away,
Found a squirrel, now we both play.

Chasing shadows, where do they go?
Is it mystery? Well, yes, you know.
Stepping on dreams, oh what a thrill,
Finding lost keys among the quill.

Secrets in the Soil

Digging deep with a rusty spoon,
Hoping to find a hidden tune.
Earthworms dance, a wiggly twist,
Uncovering snacks, oh how they missed!

Whispers flutter in the dirt,
Tales of veggies that used to hurt.
With every shovel, laughter's found,
Giggling roots make quite the sound.

Whispers of Wisdom

A wise old owl in a tree so stout,
Tells the best jokes, without a doubt.
Feathers fluffed, he guffaws so loud,
While squirrels gather, forming a crowd.

Words like acorns fall with a plop,
Hitting the ground, they bounce and stop.
One squirrel claims he knows the best,
But everyone knows he fails the test.

Thorn-laden Paths

Stumbling down a secret trail,
Tripped on brambles, I might prevail.
With every step, a prick or two,
But the giggles keep me pushing through.

Flowers bloom in hidden spots,
While I dodge those silly knots.
A comedy show, nature's jest,
Navigating paths, a wild quest.

The Mysterious Growth

In the garden, something's sprouted,
A curious plant, just the same.
With spiky arms, it waves about,
Its secrets wrapped in a prickly frame.

With every poke, a giggle slips,
A mystery wrapped in green.
What is this thing with pointy tips?
A jester's crown, or something mean?

Needles of Contemplation

A thought popped up, sharp as a needle,
Prodding minds like a playful tease.
What if life's just a wobbly steeple,
Balancing thoughts on a whimsical breeze?

We ponder hard on paths unseen,
As needles dance on a tangled line.
Is wisdom found in a wet sock's sheen?
Or in laughter shared over a glass of wine?

Prickled Insights

A few wise words, oh what a treat,
Wrapped in thorns for us to find.
Every poke whispers something sweet,
Or gives a chuckle, or often blind.

So when you prickle with your thought,
Remember humor wears a crown.
In jab and jest, wisdom is sought,
And laughter can turn the thorns upside down.

The Thorny Road to Knowing

On the path to wisdom's gate,
Every step feels like a poke.
The signs are jesters, oh, how they frustrate,
With every stumble, we just joke!

But at the end, what do we see?
A treasure chest filled with giggles and grins.
Perhaps it's not where we're meant to be,
But how we laugh while the journey begins!

Outlawed Gardens

In a plot where weeds conspire,
The flowers plot, with great desire.
Gnomes with tea, they share a tale,
Of how to make the daisies sail.

Chickens in sunglasses strut about,
Planting dreams without a doubt.
They whisper secrets to the bees,
On how to dance among the trees.

The carrots wear a fancy hat,
While potatoes stand and chat.
Together plotting in the sun,
A veggie heist, oh what a fun!

But in this patch of grand delight,
The veggies scheme to take to flight.
With rubber bands and dreams in tow,
Our outlawed garden starts to grow.

The Pulse of Natural Inquiry

A wise old owl with glasses rests,
While rabbits ponder nature's quests.
Frogs in lab coats leap and dive,
Craving answers to arrive.

The ants debate their favorite snacks,
In circles, plotting little hacks.
As butterflies note ground rules here,
"Oh don't you dare!" they quip with cheer.

Each question drips like morning dew,
A wonderland of wacky view.
Gadgets made from twigs and leaves,
Inquire if it's true what heaves.

And so they dance with questions bright,
Hypothesizing into the night.
With laughter ringing in the air,
Their pursuit shows they truly care!

Beauty in Complexity

Amidst the chaos flowers bloom,
With colors shouting in the room.
A sunflower wears polka dots,
While daisies juggle, twisting knots.

Insects argue on the best way,
To navigate this bright display.
Beetles, ants, and fluttering wings,
Compile a list of all their flings.

The cosmos spins a tangled thread,
Where whimsies frolic, fears are fed.
Petals pose with silly grins,
Embracing what the chaos spins.

Each misfit finds a place to shine,
Together crafting a design.
In this odd squad, they all agree,
Complexity brings joy, you see!

The Briar's Embrace

Wrapped in green, a secret dance,
Where vines entwine and twirl by chance.
The brambles chuckle with glee,
As critters try to climb the tree.

A hedgehog rolls in rustic style,
While squirrels keep a cheeky smile.
The briar's arms can hold so tight,
Creating hugs both day and night.

A thumping beat, the rhythm flows,
As wildflowers bloom from their toes.
Each thorn, a joke, a playful tease,
In this embrace of leafy cheese.

So join the party, lose your fear,
With every twist the fun is near.
For in this thicket of delight,
There's always room for sheer delight.

Petals of Thought

A dandelion dreams of flight,
While the crow mocks it, day and night.
Holding theories like loose change,
Bouncing ideas, feeling strange.

With a wink and a twist of fate,
Butterflies dance, they won't be late.
Where did logic take a nap?
In the garden, where plants yap.

Petals tickle the mind's spine,
All theories on a wobbly line.
Each bloom a riddle, light and brief,
A laugh, perhaps? A hint of grief.

So pluck a thought from the ground,
Comedy blooms, absurdity found.
In a pot of clay, theories hide,
But watch them grow with laughter wide.

Unraveled Notions

In a tangled garden, thoughts unwind,
Worms debate, are they of the kind?
A pointy plant speaks like a bard,
Laughing at his own backyard.

With ne'er a notion cut and dry,
A hedgehog sings of reasons why.
In crazy rhymes, ideas play,
Chasing squirrels all the day.

Each notion hops like frogs in rain,
Wet ideas with a splash of pain.
Logic slips, a slippery eel,
Wrapped in giggles, what's the deal?

So bring your quirks and take your seats,
Amongst the jests, where laughter meets.
Forget the rules, let chaos thrive,
In this garden, we're all alive!

Shadows of Belief

Behind the wall of blush and green,
Wisps of thoughts that rarely seen,
A shadow chuckles, takes a peek,
At theories that are far too meek.

In the twilight, doubts amorphous,
All swirl around, quite amorous.
A moth's debate with a bright light,
Who's to say which one is right?

The sun begins to question why,
The shadows grin, and give a sigh.
Dancing secrets in the breeze,
Witty whispers bounce through the trees.

So offer doubts a cup of tea,
Hear the laughter, wild and free.
For in the shadows, truths can twist,
And playful musings can't be missed!

Barbed Reflections

Mirrors laugh with jagged edges,
Witty rants near thorny hedges.
What reflections dare to stray,
In a garden gone a-frolic play?

With bubbles floating, thoughts collide,
A cactus nods, it won't subside.
Juggling theories like some fruit,
Barbs of wisdom, how acute!

Peering through a prickly lens,
Where laughter sparks and logic bends.
All barbed wires have tales to spin,
Of tangled thoughts that dare to grin.

So don your hat and join the game,
Where thoughts are wild and laughs are flame.
In every prick, a story stings,
And wisdom laughs as freedom sings!

Flourishing Confusion

In the garden of whims, bees dance about,
Mismatched socks and hats, who knows what they're about?
A flower's a thought that grew way too wild,
Tangles of laughter, the logic beguiled.

Cats wear capes, and dogs don crowns,
In this circus of whims, no one wears frowns.
A sunbeam slips in, as shadows, they tease,
Plant all the nonsense and grow it with ease.

The Wild Dance of Ideas

Ideas prance around in a conga line,
Salsa with concepts, a twist of the spine.
Each thought wears a feather, a hat that won't stay,
They flip and they twirl, in a whimsical sway.

One suggests rainbows, another a pie,
A sweet-tooth debate, oh my, oh my!
With giggles and snorts, they jostle and play,
Creating a jigsaw of nonsense and sway.

Cuts and Colors

A canvas of chaos, palette of cheer,
Brush strokes of mayhem, what's this over here?
Doodles turn lively in a whirl of delight,
Painted confessions that dance through the night.

Chop up the serious, mix in some fun,
Sprinkle on giggles, oh look, we've just won!
Slice through the jest, with a wink and a grin,
In this vivid mayhem, together we spin.

Coniferous Contemplations

Pine trees ponder with a crooked smile,
Debating if squirrels should talk for a while.
What sound do they make when they chatter at ease?
Oh, listen closely, it's sure to bring glee!

Beneath the green crowns, ideas take flight,
Whispering secrets through day and through night.
Philosophers giggle, the wisdom they seek,
Hints of absurdity, wrapped snugly and sleek.

The Bittersweet Fragrance of Truth

A hedgehog strolls with flair,
Sniffing out the fragrant air.
In gardens where we play and poke,
He's searching for the best of smoke.

He lifts his nose, oh what a scent!
With giggles loud, we all lament.
For every whiff of sweet delight,
A prickly truth is brought to light.

Blossoming Ideas

In a pot of jellybeans,
Reside our quirky dreams, it seems.
With jelly thoughts and candy schemes,
They bounce about in giggly beams.

One sprout a bonbon, bold and round,
Another's sweet, but just confound.
Oh, let them bloom, they have their say—
In our wild minds they dance and play!

Threads of Ambivalence

A puppet show of thoughts and doubt,
Where every string is pulled about.
The laughter trails with each new twist,
Ambivalence, how can we resist?

Oh, what a riot, this tangled web,
Of thoughts that dance on every ebb.
The left hand claps while right hand waves,
In a circus of the mind, it braves!

Grit and Gnosis

In the kitchen of the wise,
Mix emotions with a side of fries.
A dash of spice, a sprinkle of fun,
Stirred just right, we laugh and run.

With all these flavors, we taste the day,
Gritty truths in a quirky way.
Savor each bite, don't let it slip,
For every drop, there's joy to sip!

Fiery Bloomscapes

In a garden where jokes grow high,
The petals dance like a pie in the sky.
Sunshine giggles, while shadows sly,
As bees can't stop their butterfly spy.

We watered dreams with hopes and cheer,
But weeds tell stories we long to steer.
Each prickly laugh is one we hold dear,
In this wild patch of sun-soaked veneer.

Festering Notions

A thought popped up, all wiggly and queer,
Like a mushroom laughing with too much beer.
With every tickle, it danced without fear,
Creating chaos that we all cheer.

The daisies served tea with smiles so wide,
While the sun wore a hat, oh what a ride!
Strange little thoughts we can't quite abide,
Bursting with nonsense we try to hide.

Starbursts of Complexity

In a stellar field of overthought dreams,
Logic escapes through silly streams.
Each twinkling star, a joke that beams,
Unraveling knots that rip at the seams.

The universe dances with cosmic flair,
While planets giggle in saltwater air.
Confusion spins in a wild carousel,
As gravity chuckles, "What a hard sell!"

Unexpected Gardens

Amidst the paths of curvy delight,
Plants wear glasses to make things right.
The corn gets cheeky, with ears so bright,
Under the moon's soft, glowing light.

A pickle trees whispers, "Life's not so bad,"
While daisies plot to make the sun mad.
With each burst of laughter, the soil feels glad,
In this wacky patch of wild and rad.

The Raucous Blossom

In the garden, flowers poke,
Dancing wildly, laughing folk.
Petals sharp, yet joys collide,
Prickly smiles they cannot hide.

Bumblebees with dizzy spins,
Hover close, where chaos begins.
Silly stems sway left and right,
Making fun of morning light.

Witty blooms with secrets laugh,
Nature's pranksters on their path.
Sprouting quirks in every hue,
Creating joy, now who knew?

Amidst the jest, the weathers change,
Jubilant green in all its range.
Laugh aloud, let cheerful surges,
Make the most of all life's urges.

Haunting the Hedge

In shadows where the brambles lurk,
Spooky whispers, playful smirk.
Goblins dance with every breeze,
Beneath the gnarled, twisty trees.

A hedge of tales both old and new,
Charming ghosts in a verdant cue.
They debate the prick of fate,
Laughing loudly, it's never late.

Sassy vines weave cunning plots,
As creatures play and time forgot.
Fluffy clouds join in the tease,
Tickled by the rustling leaves.

While echoes chase their clever game,
Each corner holds a cheeky name.
So wander forth, don't be misled,
Join the fun, where few have tread!

Hued Perspectives

Bright colors splash with quirky flair,
Every shade a moment rare.
Laughter echoes off the grass,
As squirrels quickly run and pass.

Pink and yellow, purple twirls,
A joyful sight for boys and girls.
Sunny daisies wave with glee,
As if they're shouting, "Come and see!"

Thoughts collide in shades so bold,
Nature's secrets, yet untold.
A laugh erupts from a green sprout,
While blooms dance with a silly shout.

So lift your gaze, find joy in sight,
A swirl of shades brings pure delight.
In this wild and vivid spree,
Life's a canvas, just let it be!

Pondering Among Petals

Curious blooms with questions bright,
Whisper softly, day and night.
What if flowers had a voice?
They'd giggle, shout, make us rejoice.

In a circle, petals shout,
"What's the secret? What's it about?"
With buzzing bees to ponder too,
Together they'd muse on what is true.

A cheeky gust of wind will tease,
As thoughts drift on the playful breeze.
Petals nodding, sharing dreams,
In the garden's wildest schemes.

So join the chat and lose your fears,
With laughs and blooms, we'll share our cheers.
Beneath the sun, with hearts aglow,
We'll ponder life, while flowers grow.

Dreaming in Dusk

In shadowed fields where giggles dwell,
The whispers of mischief weave their spell.
Bugs in bow ties dance near the night,
While fireflies chuckle in the fading light.

Breeze carries puns on a playful quest,
As owls take flight in their Sunday best.
Stars wink at chatter, oh what a sight,
In the strange silence that laughs with delight.

The Thorny Path of Inquiry

With branches that poke and theories that tease,
Explorers stumble on the roots of unease.
Each prickly fact yields a curious grin,
As minds wander freely, oh where to begin?

A riddle here, a riddle there,
Cosmic quirks are found everywhere.
In questing hearts, oh how they play,
Turning pricks into giggles along the way!

Untamed Hypotheses

Unruly thoughts bounce like a frog,
In a puddle of questions, where do they slog?
Each leap brings laughter, each splash a cheer,
In a world where nonsense is perfectly clear.

Frolicking ideas like butterflies soar,
With tails of giggles, they flit and explore.
Chasing the sun, with joyfully glee,
Dancing on whims, forever free!

Stems of Consideration

In gardens of pondering, ideas sprout,
With roots in humor and laughter stout.
Petals of thoughts in vibrant bloom,
As curiosity teases in the sunny room.

Bumblebees humming, sharing a jest,
Pollinate dreams with a playful zest.
Every stem tells a tale of delight,
In the merry madness that tickles the night.

Woven in Skepticism

In a world where doubts grow wide,
Lies wear hats but can't abide.
We weave our thoughts in tangled thread,
Skepticism sings from what's unsaid.

With every twist, a chuckle hides,
Conspiracies ride on slippery tides.
The more we dig, the funnier it gets,
Unearthing truths that no one forgets.

Where logic dances in clownish shoes,
And knowledge juggles its whacky views.
Each question sparks with laughter's glow,
In minds where silliness starts to flow.

So raise a glass to rabbit holes,
To all the jokes that fill our scrolls.
For in this web of thoughts combined,
We find the joy in being blind.

Brambles of Truth

A forest thick with prickly lines,
Where secrets crawl and wisdom shines.
Navigating paths both sharp and sly,
We laugh at truths that dance and fly.

The brambles tease with every turn,
While giggles bloom and lessons burn.
In a tangle of weeds, we lose control,
And every thorn plays a minor role.

An echo bounces through this maze,
As puzzlement sets our minds ablaze.
Here, absurdity blooms with pride,
Amongst the thorns, we take a ride.

With every twist, a whimsy pops,
Unruly vines and crooked hops.
We find the truth in playful jest,
A riddle wrapped in laughter's chest.

Chasing Shadows

In a chase with shadows, we trip and fall,
Where nothing sits quite right at all.
Each playful flicker, a tease, a jest,
The silliness puts our minds to rest.

As shadows dance and run away,
We follow tales of night and day.
The jokes we crack, mere echoes bright,
In the fading glow of twilight's light.

With every step, we chase the sun,
Through fields of mirth, we dance and run.
For every shadow has a punchline near,
A giggle waiting, loud and clear.

So let us frolic, leave fears behind,
In this silly race where laughs unwind.
For in the folly of chasing dreams,
We find the humor in silly schemes.

Enigmatic Blooms

Among the blooms of curious hues,
Each petal whispers quirky news.
With every scent, a riddle plays,
Delightfully odd in mischievous ways.

The flowers giggle under the sun,
In their own language, they have fun.
Petals twist and tickle the air,
As wittiness grows with every stare.

Through gardens wild where oddities sprout,
We ponder life and twist about.
For wisdom hides in floral jest,
A bloom of laughter that feels the best.

In enigmatic patches, secrets dwell,
Each bloom a joke, a quirky spell.
So stop and smell the laughter's breeze,
Among these blooms, we find our ease.

Invasive Thoughts

In my mind grows a weed, so sly,
It tickles my brain, oh me, oh my!
I prune and I trim, but it flourishes bold,
With ideas that bounce, never turning to gold.

It whispers sweet nonsense, a tickle and tease,
A jumble of giggles, an urge to please.
I chase after reason, but it roams free,
Like a cat in the garden, laughing at me.

Sometimes it shouts with a cackle and cheer,
Dressing in theories, once far and near.
I nod and I ponder, then roll my eyes wide,
As this silly notion takes me for a ride.

But alas, my dear mind, you tricky little sprout,
You hide all the good sense, then dance all about.
What fun to be lost in this whimsical maze,
Where thoughts go to frolic and laughter stays ablaze.

The Blooming Enigma

A puzzle does blossom, its petals like jokes,
Beneath the bright sun, it winks and it pokes.
I scratch my poor head, in a state of delight,
Wondering who planted this riddle in sight.

It flashes with colors so loud and so bold,
Each hue like a secret, a story retold.
A giggle of science, a chuckle of art,
It's growing its roots right inside my heart.

This flower, it dances on tips of its toes,
While sharing the tales of where wonder goes.
Its laughter, contagious, spreads wide like a net,
Bringing smiles and questions I've never upset.

With each blooming season, I chase the unclear,
The enigma I follow, with joy and with cheer.
For in every petal lies wisdom's sweet spark,
Igniting my spirit and lighting the dark.

Barbs of Knowledge

With wisdom like cacti, prickly and bright,
Each quip has a jab, a comical bite.
I reach for the facts, but ow, there it goes,
A poke to my ego, where laughter still grows.

I gather my thoughts like rare little blooms,
Yet tangle in theories that fill crowded rooms.
They tickle my brain while they dance on the edge,
A merry-go-round of ideas I pledge.

In this garden of notions, I stumble and trip,
On thoughts that are sharp, making learning a quip.
But oh, the delight in this humorous strife,
As wisdom wraps me in its playful life.

So bring on the barbs and the giggles they spawn,
For every mistake is a chance to move on.
In laughter, we flourish, in jokes, we grow real,
With edges so funny, they sharpen the feel.

The Wretched Elegance

In a garden of chaos, weeds wear their crowns,
Dancing like royalty, while nobody frowns.
Their prickly attire, a sight to behold,
With sass in each leaf, they're daring and bold.

Picnics interrupted by nature's jest,
As the bravest of souls face their leafy quest.
Who knew that sharp edges could tickle the ribs?
A floral parade where everyone fibs!

Blossoms in battle, the colors collide,
An arboreal circus, a wild countryside.
Chasing the picnic, they plot and they scheme,
Nature's own jester, a riotous dream!

Let laughter bloom where thorns learn to grin,
In this garden of chaos, let the antics begin!
Nature's odd comedy, we can't look away,
As wretched and lovely they frolic and play.

Kites of Epiphany

In the fields where ideas take flight,
A wild breeze whispers, 'Let's now take a bite!'
Kites made of paper, dreamers in tow,
Soaring high, tangled thoughts down below.

The paper unfolds with a whimsy surprise,
As sticky wrong notions attempt to advise.
We chuckle and stumble, our minds on a spree,
As clouds mock our ponderings floating with glee.

Questioning logic while daring to drift,
Each tug of the string is a curious gift.
With laughter our compass, we wander afar,
In this jumbled delight, we're all rising stars!

So take to the skies with your fanciful chest,
Let awkward ideas find their very own zest.
In this colorful fest, let the kites dance and wave,
For it's us quirky dreamers that the winds will save.

Unruly Petals

Petals in sneakers, they're racing around,
With no sense of order, they're split on the ground.
A conga line forms with the daisies and more,
While tulips argue who's first on the floor.

Anemones giggle, "We're wild and untamed!"
The roses, all pricked, feel a bit too ashamed.
In chaos, they twirl with no plans in the air,
A floral fiesta with too much to share.

The gardener sighs as the petals all prance,
While bees form a band for the wild flower dance.
"Will you please settle down?" he pleads with a grin,
But the blossoms just chuckle, "This is where we win!"

So here's to the blooms that refuse to adhere,
With every wild twist, they'll set the mood cheer.
In the jumble of colors, they find their delight,
For nothing's more funny than nature's big fight.

Artistry in Adversity

In the land of misfits, the paint drips askew,
Creating a masterpiece, vibrant and new.
When things don't align, just smile and adjust,
For chaos invites creativity's trust.

The canvas is wrinkled, much like our days,
Yet every odd splatter ignites playful ways.
With brush strokes of laughter, let mischief unfold,
Embrace every bump, let the story be told.

From the chaos of colors, a pattern will bloom,
As we juggle the paint and banish the gloom.
In awkward arrangements, we find our own flair,
Painting life's canvas with vigor and care.

So next time it falters, your sketch of intend,
Remember the joy that arises from bends.
In every mishap, let your spirit ascend,
For true artistry thrives when we just make amends.

The Nature of Queries

In the garden of questions, things grow wild,
With petals of curiosity, brightly styled.
Some sprout in the sun, others hide in the shade,
Searching for answers, a grand charade.

A butterfly whispers, 'What's with the fuss?'
While a snail takes its time, riding on the bus.
The bees hum along, sweet tunes in the air,
Chasing pollen dreams without a single care.

Oh, the tangled vines of inquiries sprout,
Some make us chuckle, others make us doubt.
With laughter as soil, laughter as light,
We dance with ideas, oh what a sight!

So next time you're stuck in the brain's big mess,
Remember the garden is meant to impress.
Ask whatever comes; let your thoughts fly free,
In the nature of questions, we all find glee.

Velvet and Vexation

Dressed in velvet gowns, ideas take flight,
Swirling and twirling in the soft moonlight.
But some get all tangled, a real fashion crime,
Vexation's the theme, oh how they chime!

A catwalk of thoughts in mismatched shoes,
Stumbling on logic, what a funny muse!
With velvet drapes falling, and ideas askew,
We can't help but laugh at this colorful view.

Each thread tells a story, each fabric a tease,
Some whispers of brilliance, while others just freeze.
Yet we sashay on, silly smiles wide,
In the ball of absurd where our quirks become pride.

So spin those ideas, let them flow and bounce,
For in this crazy ball, we all got to pounce.
With velvet and vexation, let's raise a cheer,
To the wild, wacky wonders that bring us near!

Tangled Ideas

Knots in the brain, what a playful mess,
Ideas like spaghetti, they twirl and they press.
With forks made of dreams, we slurp them up fast,
In this noodle of thought, we're forever cast.

A jumbled up tangle of thoughts on a spree,
Like kittens at play, swatting minds with glee.
Each thread that they chase leads to a bright spark,
In the laughter of chaos, we light up the dark.

Yet there's a delight in this muddled affair,
Like a jigsaw puzzle with pieces laid bare.
Each twist and each turn brings a chuckle or two,
In the dance of our brains, oh what fun to pursue!

So let's serve up our thoughts on a plate of delight,
With a side of good humor to sweeten the night.
In tangled ideas, we find our best play,
With laughter as sauce, we'll savor the day!

Anemone of Wisdom

In the depths of the sea, wisdom sways free,
An anemone laughs at the things we decree.
It tickles the fishes as they swim by the shore,
With nudges and giggles, wanting knowledge galore.

What's life but a joke with a punchline so neat?
Anemone grins at our silly retreat.
"Why worry so much?" it gently implies,
Just float with your thoughts and enjoy the surprise!

Each wave brings a thought, a riddle, a spark,
In this underwater world, we play in the dark.
With bubbles of laughter that burst into air,
We dive into wisdom, we'll float without care.

So join in the fun, let the currents align,
In the anemone's garden, we're all on cloud nine.
With jokes from the ocean, we'll catch every tide,
In the dance of aware, we're all on this ride!

The Spine of Inquiry

In the garden of questions, we plant our seeds,
Watered with laughter, we grow our weeds.
Strange blooms of knowledge twist and twine,
Each petal a riddle, a puzzling line.

We dig and we pry, with spades made of dreams,
Beneath the surface, where nothing is as it seems.
Roots intertwine in ridiculous knots,
A comedy of errors, but we've got our plots!

As the sun sets on bright absurdity,
We dance with our findings, a strange jubilee.
With hats made of whimsy, who needs a club?
Join the party of odd ones, it's quite the hub!

In the end, we find joy in the freakish sight,
The spine of inquiry bends with delight.
Each twist of our minds, a tumble and roll,
In this zany journey, we've reached our goal!

Grotesque Beauty

In shadows of gardens, where weirdness grows,
Lies beauty outlandish, in mismatched clothes.
A frightful bouquet, grotesque and loud,
Yet somehow it catches the eye of the crowd.

Petals like smiles, yet fanged like a grin,
Unruly charm sees the oddness within.
A dance of the strange, as we twirl and spin,
This carnival blooms where the madness begins.

Amongst tangled vines, the oddities bloom,
Each leaf whispers secrets—a wild costume.
With laughter as petals, we'll dress up our fears,
In this whimsical garden, absurdity cheers.

So toast to the curious, the beautiful wights,
In laughter, we find joy in peculiar sights.
Grotesque their appearance, but sweet as can be,
In this circus of nature, we're wild and free!

Gnarled Pathways

The pathways are twisted, a curious trail,
Winding like giggles, they never go stale.
Around every corner, a riddle awaits,
With humor and chaos, the mind celebrates.

Through thickets of nonsense, we stumble and trip,
Each misstep a chuckle, an accidental flip.
Over roots like philosophers' questions that sprout,
The journey's the punchline, so laugh it out loud!

Branches are waving, "Come join us, dear mate!"
With leaves that are chattering, we'll never be late.
A gnarled delight where the curious roam,
In the woods of the silly, we're never alone.

With each twist and turn, we gather our crew,
In a maze of the mad, there's always something new.
Don't fret on the journey, just enjoy the ride,
For it's laughter and folly that'll be our guide!

The Art of Dissent

In the gallery of grumbles, we paint with our quirks,
With strokes of rebellion, each oddity lurks.
A canvas of chatter, vibrant and bold,
The art of dissent is a sight to behold.

From brushes of mischief, the colors collide,
Each splash tells a story where giggles reside.
In the realm of the quirky, we plot and we scheme,
Creating contraptions from the silliest dream.

"Why so serious?" says the clown on the wall,
With a wink and a jest, he breaks down the stall.
The voices come crashing like waves on the shore,
In this whimsical ruckus, we all want more!

So gather your crayons, unleash every thought,
In this funny dissent, we'll share what we've got.
With a splash and a giggle, the world isn't grim,
In this art that we make, joy dances on a whim!

Wildflower Whispers

In a field of bright confusion,
Petals argue on the breeze.
One thinks it's pure delusion,
The other says, "Do as you please!"

Bugs in bow ties take a stand,
Debating pollen on a whim.
They host a circus, oh so grand,
With blooms that dance and brightly swim.

Laughter drips from honey jars,
As bees tell tales of nectar's tale.
One day they'll drive their tiny cars,
And leave behind a flowered trail.

So, gather 'round and lend an ear,
To the jests of petals in the sun.
For in this plot, there's cheer, my dear,
As every joke is truly fun!

Conundrums in Bloom

A dandelion had a thought,
"Is it a weed or flower bright?"
The tulip said, "You're overwrought,
Just bloom and let them all take flight!"

A ponderosa pine stepped in,
With needles sharp, it spoke with glee,
"Life's too short to frown or grin,
Just sip the sunshine, let it be!"

Frogs in laughter croaked their tune,
While squirrels shared their nutty dreams.
In every shadow, past the moon,
The garden's full of funny schemes!

So chase away your woes and fright,
For blooms are here to make you grin.
In every crease of day and night,
There's laughter waiting to begin!

The Garden of Dilemmas

In a patch of tangled thought,
Carrots debate with chives,
"Which way should we grow?" they fought,
As the rose rolls her eyes and strives.

Sunflowers shout, "Let's reach for stars!"
But marigolds just giggle deep.
The squash says, "No, we must stay ours,
And guard our secrets while we sleep!"

A wayward bee buzzes close,
Proposing a dance of sweet romance.
"Let's plant a Kazoo, just for a dose,
And fill the air with jolly chance!"

In this bed of quirky green,
Where nothing ever goes to plan,
The laughter echoes, bright and keen,
In a riddle that just won't be ran!

Barbs and Beliefs

Cacti wear a prickly hat,
Declaring, "Life is all a game!"
The daisies laugh, "Oh, imagine that,
Do you even feel the same?"

With a shrug, the thorns conspire,
To spin a tale that's wild and bold.
While blooms, in colors, never tire,
Whisper secrets, softly told.

Dusty paths hear quirks of fate,
As roses twirl with charming grace.
While bumblebees just can't wait,
To join the fray in this sweet space.

So when you wander through this lot,
Remember that the jest does grow.
In barbs of life, find what you've sought,
And dance with laughter as you go!

Moments Between the Thorns

Amidst the prickles, laughter blooms,
A jester's cap in nature's rooms.
We dance around what stings us so,
In a garden where the wild things grow.

With each poke a chuckle escapes,
As we dodge the leafy shapes.
Nature's jesters, bold and spry,
Laughing at the poke that says goodbye.

In this wild patch, we play and blink,
Finding joy where most would sink.
A tickle here, a jab there too,
What fun we find in this leafy view.

Prickly Whispers

Listen close, the whispers tease,
In the rustling leaves that sway with ease.
A poke here, a grin so wide,
Nature's punchline, we cannot hide.

Giggles rise as branches sway,
What's sharp today can fade away.
Tell a tale with every sting,
The humor in the prickle's fling.

As shadows dance in evening's light,
We chuckle at the silly sight.
With every jab, a story's spun,
In a world where the laughs weigh a ton.

The Garden of Paradox

In a patch where opposites grow,
Soft seeds hide 'neath thorns in row.
Contradictions add to the fun,
A duel of stature when day is done.

We tiptoe lightly on prickle tips,
Hoping for joy and ignoring slips.
In this mix where chaos roams,
We find laughter in far-off homes.

The sweetest fruit's beside the woe,
With every poke, we learn and grow.
A dance of jest beneath the sun,
In paradox, we find our fun.

Spirals of Uncertainty

Round and round, we chase the buzz,
Where questions rise and fall, just because.
A twist of fate in every turn,
With each misstep, there's more to learn.

In this maze of trip and giggle,
We roll with life, and joy's the wiggle.
A sprout of nonsense, up it goes,
Society's poke, a prank it sows.

With every loop, fresh laughter brews,
A mystery in every cue.
Stumbling forth in spirals tight,
We laugh aloud, embracing the light.

Misunderstood Flora

In the garden, blooms abound,
Yet some are feared, and frowned around.
With spiky crowns and prickly jokes,
They crack us up, these funny folks.

A sunflower with a sideways grin,
Wonders where the bees have been.
"Is it my looks?" it cries, forlorn,
"I'm just a flower, not a thorn!"

Petunias roll their eyes so wide,
As daisies bicker, prideful, tried.
The poppies laugh in shades of red,
While violets plot how to get fed.

But in this patch, strange tales unfold,
Of blooms that shimmer, bright and bold.
They dance beneath the moonlit blue,
Misunderstood, but always true.

Gumbo of Questions

In a pot of swirling spice,
Questions bubble, not so nice.
What if rainbows tasted sweet?
And how can we make time repeat?

With clumps of longing and grains of doubt,
Mix in worries, stir about.
If laughter's just a fleeting thing,
Then why does joy make our hearts sing?

A pinch of dreams and zest of fear,
Let's boil them down, bring cheer near!
Is it the heat or a gentle breeze,
That tickles our fancy and makes us tease?

As flavors dance in a frothy swirl,
The pot simmers, and visions twirl.
In this gumbo, we'll all find,
A recipe that's one of a kind.

The Pulse of the Unspeakable

Whispers linger in the air,
Invisible beats, no one's aware.
A tickle here, a flutter there,
The unsaid jokes dance everywhere.

With every giggle, a secret known,
This pulse of laughter can't be shown.
Do you feel it? Tap your feet!
It's the rhythm where absurdity meets.

Knock, knock jokes that never land,
Falling flat like a timid band.
Yet still they play, all out of tune,
In the chorus of a laughing moon.

As shadows stretch, the fun unfolds,
In these vibes, pure gold is molded.
So march to the beat, oh what a thrill!
In the unspeakable, find the skill.

Garden of Whimsy

In a garden where nonsense grows,
The daisies play tag, striking poses.
Giggling lilies wave hello,
While sneaky moss takes a bow, quite low.

Underneath a laughing sky,
A crabapple claims it can fly.
With wings of leaves, it twirls and dives,
Here in whimsy, anything thrives.

Wobbling pumpkins tell tall tales,
Of quirky quests and gusty gales.
While carrots don goggles, oh so neat,
Ready to race with their veggie feet.

Laughter bubbles from every stem,
In this place that's a playful gem.
So come along, be part of the fun,
In the garden where all can run!

Prickly Reflections

In a garden full of spikes, oh what a sight,
The flowers whisper secrets that just don't feel right.
With laughter and jabs, they poke at my mind,
Reflecting on places where no peace I find.

I danced with the weeds, feeling quite bold,
Wearing a crown made of stories untold.
Each poke and each prod, a joke takes its flight,
In the thicket of nonsense, I'll stay up all night.

Crowns of Uncertainty

A king on his throne made of prickly dread,
Wants wisdom from peasants who sleep on the bed.
They shout out their theories, all wild and absurd,
While he sips on confusion, the joke's left unheard.

With crowns made of doubts, they dance in a trance,
Each step is a puzzle, an odd kind of dance.
In the kingdom of chaos, they frolic and sway,
As logic runs screaming, "I'm done for the day!"

Nature's Paradox Unraveled

In a world where the odd meets the points of a thorn,
Nature chuckles softly; it yawns and it scorns.
With riddles wrapped tight in a blanket of green,
Who knew that the lumpy could carry such sheen?

A flower that bites, what a curious sight,
Teasing philosophers well into the night.
As they ponder and scratch their perplexed little heads,
Nature roars laughter; "Go back to your beds!"

Spines of Thought

When pondering life with a frown and a pout,
A rose caught a thought, and it wriggled about.
With spines for a pen and petals for ink,
It scribbles my worries while I sit and think.

Each idea gets tangled, a jumbled cascade,
A harvest of jest where my worries do fade.
In the garden of giggles, my troubles I toss,
Embracing the chaos, with humor, not loss.

Between the Iridescent and the Rigid

In gardens where rainbows clash with old bricks,
A cat in a hat giggles at pricks.
The flowers wear shades, quite out of their style,
While bees sip their tea with a comical smile.

Around the corner, a jester of light,
Does cartwheel tricks in the shimmering night.
He bumps into clouds, they puff up and sigh,
While the moon just chuckles, oh my, oh my!

A dance of the strange, a twist in the tale,
As squirrels in bowties set sail on a trail.
With acorns for anchors, and laughter for sails,
They venture where logic just whimsically fails.

So join in the fun, step lively, take heed,
For life is a circus with whimsical creed.
Let's toast to the quirks, the giggles we find,
In the spaces between, where the silly unwind.

Echoes of the Unsaid

In a room full of whispers, the echoes collide,
A sock puppet argues with wisdom denied.
A parrot on perch squawks secrets quite bold,
While the sage in the corner sleeps snug in his fold.

With grapes worn as hats, and cucumbers too,
Veggies discuss what the veggies all knew.
They talk of the whispers that never took flight,
And giggle at dreams that escaped in the night.

The laughter grows louder, spills out of the door,
As a knobby old pumpkin starts to dance on the floor.
He tells us tales, of what could have been said,
While everyone marvels at where he has led.

In echoes of silence, where humor does reign,
The strange little stories keep teasing the brain.
So laugh at the void, where nonsense does play,
Unsaid things are treasures that brighten our day.

Twisted Fates and Fractured Insights

In a realm where pencils draw crooked designs,
A paperclip hero forges bold lines.
He fights with a stapler, a foe of great might,
In a battle of wits beyond day and night.

The rulers complain, they're measuring life,
While scissors cut ties with a twist of strife.
They argue and prance on a desk of delight,
Each squabble a jest, each jab a sheer bite.

Upon an old schmauser, two erasers debate,
Who'll save all the blunders from unfolding fate.
With giggles of graphite, their banter ensues,
In this paper-backed world, where laughter imbues.

Through chaotic designs and insights all spun,
They navigate puddles of wit, oh what fun!
In the arms of absurdity, let logic take flight,
For twisted fates here shimmer, all day and all night.

Tangled Muses

In a tangled-up garden where ideas grow wild,
A muse wearing slippers is laughing, beguiled.
With flowers that giggle and vines that entwine,
This chaos of thought is quite frankly divine!

The daisies debate with the cacti nearby,
Who's braver in pricks, who's fluffier why?
While butterflies argue, flapping wings bright,
Creating a ruckus that dances through light.

The gnome on the stool, with a mug full of dreams,
Sips wisdom from pots where the humor just beams.
As thoughts twist and twiddle, inventively spun,
In this silly old garden, all are welcome for fun.

So pluck the ripe nonsense, let silliness reign,
For muses with mischief invite us to gain.
In tangled distractions, where laughter is key,
Join the whims of the garden, come play, come see!

Echoes of Dilemma

In a garden of questions, I trip and fall,
Pondering wonders that baffle us all.
Is it bad luck or just my own feet?
I laugh at the thought, it's both a retreat.

With friends by my side, we chuckle and jest,
Debating the meaning of life's odd request.
Do we dance in a circle or march in a line?
The answer is vague, but at least we eat fine!

Seagulls overhead, they squawk and they screech,
Like critics of humor, they announce what they teach.
In each silly twist, there's wisdom so clear,
Laughter's the prize, let's give it a cheer!

So let's toast to our folly, with laughter and cheer,
In this playful dilemma, we've nothing to fear.
For every mishap and puzzling plight,
Makes life's curious journey a true delight!

Fractured Dreams

I once had a vision of flying so high,
With pancakes for wings, soaring past the sky.
But dreams can be quirky, like socks in the wash,
I landed on syrup – oh what a splosh!

My friend swore she saw a giraffe in the tree,
Claiming it danced with a tune, oh-so-free.
But when I looked closer, just leaves in the breeze,
Who knew imagination could tickle like bees?

We chase after wonders, bold visions we chase,
In impractical shoes, we still embrace space.
Sometimes I wonder, what's real and what's jest?
But life's greatest moments are often the best!

So here's to the silly, the fractured, the wild,
To dreaming with laughter, like a curious child.
Each twist in our journey, a treat that we find,
For fun is the cure—let's all be unconfined!

Cacti of Cognition

With thoughts like spines, they poke and they prod,
Ideas bloom brightly, even when odd.
In a patch of perplexity, we laugh and we learn,
Through prickly conundrums, our minds always churn.

A friend asked me once, 'Can time grow on trees?'
I pondered a moment, then answered with ease.
'If clocks could be fruits, they'd hang with a grin,
Still, they wouldn't taste sweet—oh where have I been?'

With sapling solutions, we giggle and think,
Filling the days with bright ink from a blink.
For every sharp thought, there's laughter to find,
In the garden of banter, all hearts are aligned!

So while life may poke us like cacti in bloom,
We gather our giggles and dance past the gloom.
With a playful perspective that's more than a phase,
We tackle each riddle with chuckles and praise!

Thorny Conundrums

Stumbled on riddles with leaves all around,
Thought I found treasure, but just twigs I found.
I searched for the answers, but they danced out of reach,
Like elusive pinatas avoiding my speech.

A puppy shows wisdom, he barks at my plight,
Inviting me over for laughs and some bites.
'Fret not,' says the pup, 'It's all in good fun!
Let's roll in this tangle until we see sun!'

From puzzled murmurs to fits of deep glee,
Our wits are a riddle, a wild jubilee!
Each thorn in the path is a tickle, it seems,
Creating the laughter that fills up our dreams.

So here's to the quirks and the fumbles we claim,
For missteps and mishaps are all part of the game.
In thorny conundrums, we rise and conclude,
That humor's the balm for the riddles they brewed!

Jagged Insights

In a garden of pricks, I sipped my tea,
Wisdom grows wild, as wild as can be.
A perplexed bee buzzed, quite out of place,
Flew into mischief, with pollen on face.

A hedgehog rolled by, with a curious glance,
Told me the secret to life's funny dance.
"Stumble and tumble, don't take it too hard,
Laughter's the engine; let's rev up the yard!"

Socks on a cactus, what a sight to see!
Footwear rebellion, in nature's decree.
Mismatched ideas, dancing 'round in my head,
Who needs a roadmap? Just follow the spread!

So I frolicked and laughed, a perplexed little sort,
In a world where the thorns become quite the sport.
With wit as my armor, I charged through the field,
Embraced all the chaos, my heart was my shield.

Briars of Understanding

In a thicket so dense, I found quite the stash,
Of ideas like briars, all tangled and brash.
An owl with glasses, so wise yet so sly,
Chortled through feathers, "Just give it a try!"

How many sharp points can one mind withstand?
I encountered a lizard, he offered a hand.
"Don't fret my friend, just wade through the mess,
For life is a riddle; embrace the distress!"

A porcupine pranced with a raucous cheer,
While humor unraveled all doubts, all fear.
Finding joy in confusion, and chaos in jest,
I learned that the briars can offer the best.

So next time you're tangled, don't wear a frown,
Just dance with the thoughts that seem thorny and brown.
With laughter your compass, you'll find every clue,
In the briars of wisdom, you'll giggle right through.

The Riddle of the Outdoors

A squirrel with sass, atop the tall pine,
Challenged my thoughts with a riddle divine.
"What's fuzzy, quite tricky, and makes everyone laugh?"
I pondered and chuckled, quite baffled by path.

With leaves that are laughing, and dirt that can sing,
The riddle unraveled like a kooky old fling.
"It's the joys of confusion, the quirks we all wear,
The silly little moments that bubble with flair!"

A raccoon with glasses chimed in with a grin,
"The answer's quite simple, let the madness begin!
For life is one riddle, all twisted and bent,
A jester's creation, on mischief it's spent!"

So frolic through forests, with giggles and glee,
Embrace all the puzzles that nature can be.
With humor your guide, you'll unravel each thread,
The riddle of life, where laughter is fed.

Fluid Realms

In a land of soft puddles where giggles collect,
The bends of reality twist and reflect.
A fish wearing glasses, quite silly and spry,
Invited me over to learn how to fly.

"Just leap from the rivers, don't worry about falls,
For laughter's the secret behind all of our walls!"
The bubbles around us began to unite,
In a splash of absurdity, morning turned bright.

A snail made a toast with a twig as his flute,
"To the merry adventures that make life so cute!"
We danced through the streams that giggled with glee,
In fluid dimensions, where fun grew like a tree.

So plunge in the laughter, let worries all breeze,
For the realms that we wander are shaped by our tease.
In this whimsical world, where antics abound,
The fluidity of joy is the treasure we've found.

Anachronistic Asides

In a garden where aged frogs jest,
Time travelers sip tea, feeling blessed.
One claims he brought sunlight from afar,
While another argues in reverse of a car.

A squirrel dashes past with a monocle,
Debating logic that's quite comical.
"Aren't we all just scribbles in sand?"
The beetle replies with a wave of his hand.

Dandelions giggle, their heads held high,
While walking sticks dance, oh my, oh my!
In this circus of prattle, the laughter climbs,
As the past collides with nonsensical rhymes.

So come take a peek at this curious scene,
Where questions abound, but answers are lean.
In the land of the curious, absurdity reigns,
And fun is the treasure, with no real gains.

The Jagged Edge of Imagination

Chasing ghosts with a lollipop held,
My thoughts fly high, like jellybeans swelled.
A cat with a cape zips by the moon,
While unicorns trumpet a silly, sad tune.

On paper planes, we sail through the stars,
In search of a land where the odd quickly spars.
"Is that a hat or a nose on a chair?"
I muse with a grin, it's quite the strange fare.

Beetles with top hats strut on the lawn,
Discussing whether the sun likes to yawn.
The sun sneers back, shining brightly instead,
As ideas collude in this whimsical spread.

Together we laugh, our thoughts intertwine,
Making much of the merry, a nonsensical line.
Here on the cusp of the wild and the wise,
We find that bright dreams come in silly disguise.

Roaming Through Riddles

A pickle danced with a riddle-tongued sage,
Who claimed absurd wisdom from every age.
"If a sandwich sings in the key of a sock,
Does it still taste good at six o'clock?"

Giggling flowers began to debate,
While gossiping pebbles tilted fate.
"A ladder to nowhere!" whispered a leaf,
As we pondered the meaning, full of disbelief.

In this zany realm of tangled delight,
Frogs wear bow ties while stars shine bright.
The trees shake with laughter; oh, what a tease,
As shadows unfold in the gentle breeze.

So merry we wander through riddle and jest,
Searching for answers that never find rest.
In laughter we find all the strange hows and whys,
Wrapped in the mystery of our curious skies.

When Blooms Collapse

Petals collide in a feathery fuss,
Claiming their stories in a hurry to rush.
"Is it Friday or Tuesday?" one tulip did shout,
As they tumbled together in colorful doubt.

The daisies protested, with sides all a-quirk,
"Let's form a band, and we'll all go to work!"
With spoons as their instruments and onions as drums,
They played all their anthems with flowered hums.

But bloom after bloom, they began to droop low,
As laughter turned quiet, and petals lay slow.
"Sometimes it hurts to giggle and muse,"
Said a rose on the edge, wearing morning dew shoes.

Yet through the collapse, they stuck out their stems,
Finding their joy in the oddest of gems.
So when blooms may collapse, remember this song,
Laughter is joy, and it helps us stay strong.

Radiance in Rubble

In the garden of chaos, weeds wear a crown,
Sunshine chuckles, as petals tumble down.
The dandelions gossip, oh what a sight,
While squirrels debate who will take flight.

A snail ambles slowly, as time takes a pause,
He's puzzled by life, and, oh, what a cause!
The flowers all dance, in mismatched attire,
Even the cacti are feeling desire.

Butterflies enter, with wings colored bright,
They jest about how they always take flight.
A ladybug winks, and they all get along,
In this carnival chaos, they sing their own song.

So amidst the hilarity, laughter takes root,
In a world where quirkiness seems absolute.
Rubble and radiance twirl in the breeze,
Life is a party, and that's sure to please.

Petals of Perception

In the meadow of madness, a flower turns red,
It claims to be rare, with a snobby head.
The daisies all giggle, sneezing pollen with glee,
As they ponder the weight of philosophy.

The bees buzz with wisdom, though they skip the class,
"Why think too much? Just enjoy the grass!"
A daffodil nods, with a swagger so bold,
Saying, "Life's just a joke, and I'm living gold!"

Underneath all the petals, a snail spouts a verse,
"Why worry about truths? Isn't nonsense diverse?"
The wind shakes its head, with a laugh in its swirl,
While the poppies respond, "Life's a marvelous whirl!"

So let us prance lightly, with humor in bloom,
Though theories might frighten, we'll banish the gloom.
In a field full of folly, let joy take its flight,
For petals of laughter will conquer the night.

Shadows of Speculation

In a world full of whispers, the shadows convene,
Discussing their theories, though none are too keen.
A cat there observes, with a smirk on its face,
As they bicker and squabble, with flair and with grace.

"Is the moon made of cheese?" one shadow does pry,
While another replies, "I think that's a lie."
The figures debate on what sunlight could mean,
While the chickens just laugh, and cluck in between.

A shadow of doubt is flickering near,
It wonders if laughter is truly sincere.
Yet a sprite in the corner, with giggles to spare,
Proclaims that each theory is just fluff in the air.

So let's scoff at the shadows and what they believe,
In the realm of the ridiculous, let's dare to achieve.
For while they may ponder, and stumble around,
It's clearly the punchlines that always abound.

The Search for Clarity

With magnifying glasses, they seek for the truth,
As clowns juggle theories, and juggle their youth.
The search gets absurd, as logic runs wild,
While rubber chickens squawk and the whole world is styled.

A hint of confusion, like pie in the face,
As answers grow tangled, in this bewildering race.
The thinkers are spinning, like tops on a string,
While honking their noses, they don't give a fling.

"Let's ask the goldfish!" one scholar interpolates,
As they dive for opinions from old fishy mates.
With gills full of secrets, they bubble with cheer,
And suddenly, clarity seems rather near.

So in this quest for the wisdom they crave,
They navigate nonsense, like a ship on a wave.
For laughter will guide them, like stars in the night,
And clarity's shadow is wrapped in delight.

www.ingramcontent.com/pod-product-compliance
Lightning Source LLC
Chambersburg PA
CBHW072147200426
43209CB00051B/816